MY RABBIT

Me and My
PET

By William Anthony

KidHaven
PUBLISHING

Published in 2020 by KidHaven Publishing, an Imprint of Greenhaven Publishing, LLC
353 3rd Avenue, Suite 255, New York, NY 10010

This edition is published by arrangement with Booklife Publishing.

Written by: William Anthony
Edited by: Robin Twiddy
Designed by: Jasmine Pointer

Cataloging-in-Publication Data

Names: Anthony, William.
Title: My rabbit / William Anthony.
Description: New York : KidHaven Publishing, 2020. | Series: Me and my pet | Includes glossary and index.
Identifiers: ISBN 9781534533530 (pbk.) | ISBN 9781534533554 (library bound) | ISBN 9781534533547 (6 pack) | ISBN 9781534533561 (ebook)
Subjects: LCSH: Rabbits--Juvenile literature.
Classification: LCC SF453.2 A58 2020 | DDC 636.9'322--dc23

Photo credits: Images are courtesy of Shutterstock.com. With thanks to Getty Images, Thinkstock Photo and iStockphoto.
Front cover - Samuel Borges Photography, SingjaiStock. 2 - David Prado Peruchas, Happy monkey, oksana2010. 4 - Samuel Borges Photography.
5 - cameilia. 6 - Lefebvre Alain. 7 - Julija Sapic. 8 - wavebreakmedia. 9 - Steve Lovegrove. 10 - Nadezhda V. Kulagina. 11 - Zurijeta. 12 - Pixel-Shot.
13 - Inna Reznik. 14 - Milarka. 15 - rosebowl. 16 - Tyler Olson. 17 - Tatyana Vyc. 18 - Beachbird. 19 - sirtravelalot. 20 - By Shai Asor (CC BY-SA 4.0
(https://creativecommons.org/licenses/by-sa/4.0)), from Wikimedia Commons. 21 - By Shai Asor (CC BY-SA 4.0
(https://creativecommons.org/licenses/by-sa/4.0)), from Wikimedia Commons. 22 - Samuel Borges Photography. 23 - SunKids.

Printed in the United States of America

CPSIA compliance information: Batch #BW20KL. For further information contact Greenhaven Publishing LLC, New York, New York at 1-844-317-7404.

CONTENTS

Page 4   Chloe and Scotch
Page 6   Getting a Rabbit
Page 8   Home
Page 10   Playtime
Page 12   Food
Page 14   Bedtime
Page 16   The Vet
Page 18   Growing Up
Page 20   Super Rabbits
Page 22   You and Your Pet
Page 24   Glossary and Index

Words that look like this can be found in the glossary on page 24.

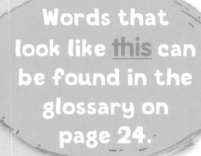

Chloe ♥ and Scotch

Hello! My name's Chloe, and this is my pet rabbit, Scotch. He's seven years old. Rabbits are my favorite animal because they are soft, friendly, and I love the way they hop!

Chloe →

Scotch →

4

Whether you're thinking about getting one, or you've had one for a little while, Scotch and I are going to take you through how to look after a rabbit!

Lead the way, Scotch!

5

Getting a Rabbit

Looking after a rabbit means you are going to take on a lot of **responsibility**. You will need to feed them, and give them a nice home with a warm bed.

Scotch's Hutch

Take your time choosing your rabbit. You will be friends for a long time!

My family got Scotch from a pet store, but you can get rabbits from lots of places. You can get them from someone who **breeds** them, or from a **rescue center**.

Home

When you first get your rabbit, you need to decide whether you will keep them indoors or outside. Rabbits can live in either place.

If you keep your rabbit outside, they'll need a hutch with lots of hay to keep warm. If you keep your rabbit indoors, make sure you hide wires and make everywhere safe!

Playtime

Rabbits are very curious (say: cure-ee-us), which means they like to explore. It's good to give them lots of things to play with. This keeps their minds busy all day long.

A comfortable rabbit is a happy rabbit!

When you're petting your rabbit, it's important to be soft and gentle with them. You might frighten them if you are <u>rough</u> with them or shout a lot!

11

Food

Hay is just grass that has dried out!

Feeding your bunny isn't too hard. Rabbits are called grazing (say: gray-zing) animals, which means they mostly eat grass and hay.

As well as grass and hay, rabbits need a little bit of **variation** (say: vare-ee-ay-shun) in their **diet**. You can buy rabbit food from a pet store.

Make sure you put some water in their bottle!

Bedtime zzᶻ

If your rabbit
lives outside in a hutch,
they will need lots of bedding to
stay warm at night. It can get very cold
in winter.

Rabbits like to sleep in lots of hay, straw, sawdust, or paper. Every rabbit will have their favorite. It's important to try out each type of bedding and see which one they like best!

The Vet

Vets are doctors, but for animals instead of humans!

Rabbits can get sick, just like humans. Rabbits that are sick can go to the vet. The vet will do everything they can to help your rabbit get better again!

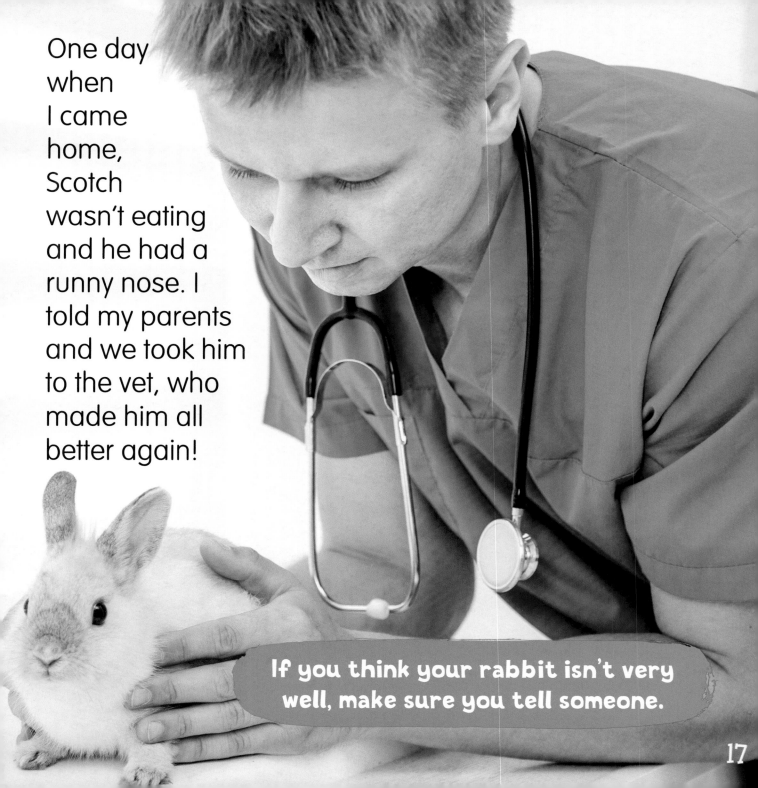

One day when I came home, Scotch wasn't eating and he had a runny nose. I told my parents and we took him to the vet, who made him all better again!

If you think your rabbit isn't very well, make sure you tell someone.

17

Growing Up

Not all rabbits live for the same amount of time. Some live for around 10 years, but others have lived to the age of 18! Keep an eye on your bunny to find out when they are getting old.

Your rabbit will sleep much more and eat much less when it is old.

Make sure older rabbits are as comfortable as possible.

When your bunny is getting old, you need to be gentle with them and give them lots of hugs. Try to get them to **exercise** as much as possible to keep them healthy.

19

Super Rabbits

All rabbits are amazing, but some bunnies are super rabbits! Bini the Bunny lives in the U.S., and he can paint his own works of art!

Bini also holds the world record for the most basketball slam dunks in one minute by a rabbit. He scored seven!

You ♥ and Your Pet

Whether your rabbit is a normal rabbit or a super rabbit, make sure you take care of them just like Scotch and I have taught you!

I'm sure you'll make a great pet owner. Have fun with your new fluffball. If you had a super rabbit, what would be the first world record you would try to break?

GLOSSARY

breed	to take care of animals in order to make more animals
diet	the kinds of food that an animal or person usually eats
exercise	to take part in physical activity to become stronger and healthier
rescue center	a place that helps animals that have had a difficult life find a new loving home
responsibility	having tasks that you are expected to do
rough	causing or likely to cause harm or injury; not gentle
variation	a change from what is normal

INDEX

beds 6, 14–15
Bini 20–21
exploring 10
grass 12–13
grazing 12

hay 9, 12–13, 15
health 19
hutch 6, 9, 14
indoors 8–9
old 4, 18–19

outside 8–9, 14
pet store 7, 13
water 13

24